My Stepdad is an Alien

David Harmer was born in 1952 on the Planet Kent, near the London nebula. At the age of thirteen his father packed all the family into a large red space rocket and flew through the starry sky, landing on a distant planet called South Yorkshire. It was very different, with strange languages and customs of its own, but David grew to love it very much. He still lives there and when he isn't a poet, he is the headteacher of a primary school in Doncaster, a small asteroid floating around the Moon of Sheffield. Because he works with young children and their teachers all day, he knows all about weird and strange alien life forms. He is married to Paula and has two daughters, Lizzie and Harriet. Their space station is filled with cats, fish, lizards and a Giant Purple Grodsplokulian from the Planet Splink.

Theresa Murfin's imaginative illustrations have been influenced by her belief from an early age that her parents were aliens and her grandparents lived on the moon. These drawings also benefit from the use of her seven arms and three heads.

Other books published by Macmillan

WHEN THE TEACHER ISN'T LOOKING
Poems chosen by David Harmer

THE VERY BEST OF DAVID HARMER
Poems by David Harmer

THE TEACHER'S REVENGE
Poems chosen by Brian Moses

YOU'RE NOT GOING OUT LIKE THAT!
Poems chosen by Paul Cookson

TAKING MY HUMAN FOR A WALK
Poems chosen by Roger Stevens

My Stepdad is an Alien

Poems chosen by **David Harmer**

Illustrated by **Theresa Murfin**

MACMILLAN CHILDREN'S BOOKS

For my dear friend Paul Cookson, with thanks

First published 2003 by Macmillan Children's Books
a division of Macmillan Publishers Limited
20 New Wharf Road, London N1 9RR
Basingstoke and Oxford
www.panmacmillan.com

Associated companies throughout the world

ISBN 0 330 41552 2

1 3 5 7 9 8 6 4 2

A CIP catalogue record for this book is available from
the British Library.

Printed and bound in Great Britain by Mackays of Chatham plc, Kent

Contents

My Stepdad is an Alien

I'd suspected for some time.
I finally got up the courage
to talk to him about it.

I think you're an alien, I told him.

Nonsense, he said. Why do you think that?

You're bald. You don't have any hair
anywhere.

That's not that unusual, he said.

Well, you've got one green eye
and one blue one.

That doesn't make me an alien, he replied.

You can make the toaster work
without turning it on.

That's just a trick, he smiled.

Sometimes I hear you
talking to Mum in a weird alien language.

I'm learning Greek
and Mum lets me practise on her.

What about your bright blue tail?

Ah, he said thoughtfully.
You're right, of course.
So, the tail gave it away, did it?

Roger Stevens

Happy Paint

My dad didn't know
I was watching
when he went out
late in the night
with his brush
and his tin of Happy Paint.
He did the whole town:
buildings, pavements – the lot.
Even Patch, our dog,
got splashed
   before running
         in to hide.

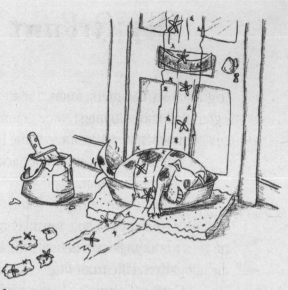

It was dark;
and everyone else
was tucked up in bed.
By morning,
rain had washed away
all his hard work.
People were their usual grumpy selves;
but Patch has been wagging his tail
ever since.

Martin Brown

My Granny

Some grannies are knitters, some grannies make hats
Some grannies smoke kippers, some grannies keep cats
Some grannies have gardens and some live in flats
But my Granny's a lumberjack
How about that!

She never stays in on a Saturday night
She goes to the woods on her big mountain bike
And she chops down the trees with a thud and a thwack
Cos my Granny's a lumberjack
How about that!

The neighbours all think that my Granny is bonkers
She goes to the forest to rummage for conkers
Then she gets out her buzz-saw and suddenly 'CRACK!'
Cos my Granny's a lumberjack
How about that!

She loves to go out when the weather is fine
And the sweet air is rich with the fresh smell of pine
As she clears up the forest with Chuck and Big Matt
Cos my Granny's a lumberjack
How about that!

Don't tell her she's old and don't tell her she's mad
Don't say all this dumb lumberjacking's a fad
Or she'll get out her buzz-saw and suddenly 'SPLAT!'
Cos my Granny's a lumberjack
How about that!

Ann Ziety

Mrs Goodwin's Part-time Job

It was just a part-time job
but the money wasn't bad
and it relieved a housewife's boredom
and stopped her going mad.
Of course it was top secret
and the family mustn't know.
She checked her space-time monitor.
It must be time to go.
'Beam me up,' she bellowed,
'the kids have gone to school,
and my husband's gone to work,
so beam me up, you fools
for the Zoorgs mass on the borders
and the Voorgs wait to attack
and I've got to save a planet
before the kids get back.'
A voice said, 'OK, Captain.
It shouldn't take a sec.'
And in a trice, foot tapping,
she was standing on the deck
of a universe class starship,
twenty kilometres wide.
'Full speed ahead, disintegrators

set to fire,' she cried.
The Voorg fleet ran in terror,
the Zoorgs thought twice and fled.
'And now let's save that planet
and the job's all done,' she said.
They beamed her down at home time
as her four kids clattered in.
She landed in the kitchen
in something of a spin
and started to peel carrots
with her space corps issue knife.
'Poor Mum,' her children cackled,
what a boring life.'

Marian Swinger

Mer-Mum

She holds a silver-backed mirror
as she brushes her long dark hair.
Her sea-green eyes grow hazy
as she croons a mournful air.

She likes to swim in the ocean
every day when I'm at school
and in the summer evenings
she rests in the goldfish pool.

She wears her pearly earrings
her skirts fall to the ground
and as she glides along the floor
the scent of seaweed's all around.

I love my mermaid mummy
and I know that she loves me.
I dread the day that
    she decides
to go back to
    the sea.

Angela Topping

There's Something Strange About Dad

He doesn't seem to be himself these days.

Spends ages gazing wistfully out of the window
Like he doesn't want to be here.

Doesn't really talk to Mum much
Or play with me or my forty-seven brothers and sisters.

Caught him watching a strange channel yesterday
– something about *fudbawl*, or *socka* . . .

Also, found a strange substance in the waste recycle unit
– a white container with the letters $P - I - Z - Z - A$

I have never heard of this planet although it seems to be a disc
with many colours and strange vegetation.

His new clothes seem strange – he says they're the latest craze
. . . *cool and trendy baby*, whatever that may mean.

I do not know the words *kipper tie* and *purple flares*.
But they look weird, like something from outer space.

No, there's something not quite
    right about Dad,
He just doesn't seem his
    normal self.

He hasn't used his third eye in ages
And his antennae seem to be on
    upside down.

His spots look smudgy, his warts
    seem to move
And he spends ages in the
    bathroom.

I'm beginning to wonder
I don't want to believe it but . . .

I think my dad could be . . . a
    human.

Paul Cookson

My Grandad

My grandad may look old and wrinkled
But crooks know he's quick and he's hard
He nabs 'em when he's undercover
When he helps out at New Scotland Yard.

My grandad's a Hollywood stuntman
He features in all the big hits
Being shot at or thrown out of airplanes
Run over, or being blown to bits.

My grandad's a hero at football
With a hat-trick in every big game
Relied on to head home the winner
He loves the crowd cheering his name.

My grandad's an MI5 agent
In countries and places afar
Gets caught up in all sorts of danger
And escapes in his top-secret car.

My grandad likes swimming with crocodiles
He's usually safe from attack
They know that if one of them bites him
My grandad will *always* bite back!

My grandad is always so busy
There's nothing that he wouldn't dare
No wonder, whenever we visit
He's always asleep
in his chair.

Martin Brown

Frogsborn

One Hallowe'en at dead of night
I heard a floorboard creak,
and crept out on the landing
to have a little peep.

My mum was up and acting strange,
in satin cape of black
and climbing through the window
she clutched a pointy hat.

She didn't have her nightie on,
the one from M & S.
I wondered where the party was –
it must be fancy dress.

Perhaps my dad, too tired to go
would rather stay in bed.
Deciding not to wake him up
I followed Mum instead.

I found her dancing in a field
with witches round a pond.
But when I sneezed she caught my eye
and flashed a silver wand.

She held a lamp
    up to my face,
a ghostly
    pumpkin grin.
She muttered
    strange and magic words
that made my poor head spin.

Into the slime-black pond I sank –
I thought that I might choke
and when I tried to call for help
it came out as a croak.

I warn you, children, hear my words
should you but hear a creak
of floorboards in the dead of night
beware! Go back to sleep.

Celia Gentles

Why?

Why does Mum look so furtive
when I ask her where she has been?
Why does she keep an old sea chest
and what does her parrot mean
when it squawks out, 'Shiver me timbers'
and 'Bring out those pieces of eight'?
Why is Mum always phoning
someone she calls the first mate,
why does she peel the potatoes
with a cutlass, a mean looking tool
and why does she wear soggy seaboots
when she comes to collect me from school?

Then why does she keep on singing,
'Yo ho ho and a bottle of rum'
and wearing that silly black eyepatch?
It's not what one expects of a mum.
And why does she bury treasure
under the pear tree at night
and why does she sometimes look
as if she's been caught in a fight?
I just haven't found any answers;
in fact I keep drawing a blank
but I'll just ask this one
     last question,
why am I walking
     the plank?

Marian Swinger

Doing What's Normal

Full moon, and the children are sleeping.
Dad puts on an old dressing gown, then slips
out of sight in the depths of the night as he
heads for the woods out of town.

He shrieks in the fields like a banshee, and
scratches on walls as he passes. He'll splash
through a stream with a rapturous scream,
then pause to wipe spray off his glasses.

With eyes glowing bright in the moonshine,
and fangs drippy-wet with saliva, he'll cause
instant fear if a human comes near, be it
tramp, vagabond or night driver.

Away from the strains of the City – a job
so demanding and formal – he gets these
attacks, but they help him relax as a werewolf,
just doing what's normal.

Barry Buckingham

Aunt Jane

My Auntie Jane is a funny old stick:
She's been alive for ever.
She likes to wear a long black dress,
a hat with a raven's feather.

Her skin is pale like marble,
her teeth are gleaming white,
her eyes are hard to fathom.
She'll go out only at night.

She chooses crimson lipstick,
pointed shoes upon her feet,
her hair is swept up high.
I've never seen her eat.

I'm not allowed to visit her
without my mum and dad:
she has some quaint old habits:
my friends think she is mad.

Her house is quaintly spooky.
It's old-fashioned, dark and cold.
She hugs me very tightly,
I can't escape her hold.

She always keeps the curtains drawn
and does not like the light,
there's not a mirror to be seen
for she claims she looks a sight.

She tells me how she loves me
She'll eat me up, she cries,
what pointed teeth my auntie has,
what terrifying eyes!

My parents say it's time to go
And wrap me in my coat
They take such special care to tie
my scarf around my throat.

They say Aunt Jane's eccentric
and is better left alone
with her spooky castle of a house,
her bed carved out of stone.

Angela Topping

The Greatest of Them All

You can keep your superheroes
Like Batman and the rest –
My dad can beat 'em all hands down,
He really is the best.

He tears up toilet tissues,
He can break a twig in two,
He can lift a bag of feathers,
No, there's nothing he can't do.

He can bend a piece of cardboard,
He can frighten new-born flies,
And at snapping off a daisy head
He always takes first prize.

He's stronger than a sparrow
And he's faster than a snail,
He can punch a hole in newspapers
And never ever fail.

He's thinner than a matchstick
And his biceps look like peas,
His legs are like a spider's
And he's got two knobbly knees.

He's a legend in his lifetime
He's a hero through and
through.
And what's the name we
know him by?
It's *Superwimp* – that's who!

Clive Webster

Dragon

A dragon lives beneath Mum's bed.
I know it does but my mum said
It's daft to say something like that.
We haven't even got a cat!
But I sneaked in there late at night
and gave myself a nasty fright!
Little puffs of smoke were seen
gliding upwards, bright pea green.
I pressed myself against the door
As strong claws scraped across the floor.
One rumble was enough for me.
I dared not have a look to see
if Mum had got herself a pet.
I'd really like to know and yet
Why does she feel she cannot share
the creatures that she keeps in there?
Of course it might outgrow the bed,
then will she keep it in the shed?
The thing that's really bothering me
Is something that my Mum can't see.
She jokes and smiles and pulls my leg,
but where'd she get a dragon egg?

Kate Boddy

My Father

Some fathers work at the office, others work at the store,
Some operate great cranes and build up skyscrapers galore,
Some work in canning factories counting green peas into cans,
Some drive all night in huge and thundering removal vans.

But mine has the strangest job of the lot.
My Father's the Chief Inspector of – What?
O don't tell the mice, don't tell the moles,
My Father's the Chief Inspector of HOLES.

It's a work of the highest
    importance because
    you never know
What's in a hole, what
    fearful thing is
        creeping from below.
Perhaps it's a hole to the ocean
    and will soon gush water in tons,
Or maybe it leads to a vast cave full of gold and skeletons.

    Though a hole might seem to have nothing but dirt in,
    Somebody's simply got to make certain.
    Caves in the mountain, clefts in the wall,
    My Father has to inspect them all.

That crack in the road looks harmless. My Father knows it's not.
The world may be breaking into two and starting at that spot.
Or maybe the world is a great egg, and we live on the shell,
And it's just beginning to split and hatch: you simply cannot tell.

    If you see a crack, run to the phone, run!
    My Father will know just what's to be done.
    A rumbling hole, a silent hole,
    My Father will soon have it under control.

Keeping a check on all these holes he hurries from morning
    to night.
There might be sounds of marching in one, or an eye
    shining bright.
A tentacle came groping from a hole that belonged to a
    mouse,
A floor collapsed and Chinamen swarmed up into the house.

    A Hole's an unpredictable thing –
    Nobody knows what a Hole might bring.
    Caves in the mountain, clefts in the wall,
    My Father has to inspect them all!

Ted Hughes

Uncle Percy's Pigeon Loft

In Uncle Percy's pigeon loft
Live birds which are not grey or soft.
They do not coo, they cannot fly,
They've never seen the sweet blue sky.

They're made of cogs and wire and string,
These metal birds which never sing.
Their beaks are barbed, their claws are worse –
They're Uncle Percy's robot curse!

Dave Ward

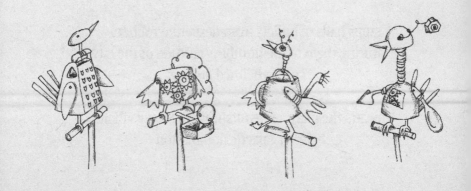

Dad's a Superhero

I know the truth about Dad.

Leaving our car behind (no need for it)
at the crack of dawn each day
Dad flies to the heart of the teeming metropolis.

There, clad in Superhero disguise, Dad:

supports collapsing bridges
just
in
the
nick
of time

to save thousands of terrified passengers on runaway trains,

stops hails of bullets from desperate robbers –
capturing them to the humble gratitude of the city's
overwhelmed police,

thwarts the plans of fiendish, alien, Super villains
bent on galactic domination

and rescues helpless kittens stranded up trees.

But Dad is Super modest and lets everyone think
he's just a hack on a local rag

but I know Dad's a Superhero

for no ordinary mortal could drag himself home
at the end of each working day as heroically tired as my
dad does.

Philip Waddell

Hush Hush

Norman is
a
secret agent.
Only family
and
close friends
know this.
Those of you
who have read
this poem
please
destroy it
and
forget
you ever
saw
it.

John C. Desmond

Grandad's Night Shift

These are the hands that hold the wheel
That drives the bus in the dead of night,
When the world's asleep, along my route
I speed with barely a soul in sight.
'Where are you going?' you might ask.
'To the end of the world,' I'd reply,
As I skim along on my sinister task
With a ghoulish look in my eye.

Redvers Brandling

Grandma's Strange Machine

An advert in a magazine
Appealed to Grandma Geraldine.
We had our doubts, but she was keen
And sent off for her strange machine.

The parts were sent from Aberdeen.
They came wrapped up in polythene
To keep them dry, rust-free and clean.
We counted them. There were umpteen.

'Quite right!' said Grandma Geraldine,
Moving an antique figurine.
'Now bring my tool-kit here, Kathleen,
And take those chairs through there, Eugene.'

Then putting on her gaberdine,
She spread a sheet of crinoline
Where all her furniture had been
And started building her machine.

Twelve hours passed . . . perhaps thirteen
When: 'Nearly done!' said Geraldine,
Screwing a grommet in between
Two sprockets on the mezzanine.

Her room now seemed a submarine
That hummed like some smooth limousine
And glowed an eerie kind of green
Which came from a computer screen.

She oiled the joints with margarine
And filled both tanks with gasoline
Then stood well back, surveyed the scene,
And said: 'I love its shiny sheen.'

We cried: 'But, Grandma Geraldine.
What do those words and numbers mean
That keep appearing on that screen?
And why've you built this strange machine?'

She paused while wiping her hands clean,
Said: 'Children, please don't intervene!'
Then climbing into her machine,
She sent us home . . . 'Where have you been?'

Our parents asked. 'At Geraldine's,'
We said, explaining what we'd seen
And all about her strange machine,
Its sounds, its smells, its bright green screen.

Well, years have passed. I'm now nineteen.
Flats were built where her house had been.
It disappeared. We've not since seen
Or heard one word from Geraldine.

Nick Toczek

When the Children Turn Their Backs

Mum and Dad know where it's at
A bit of this and a bit of that
They do more than have their chats
When the children turn their backs

Scattered toys in seconds flat
It's a change of habitat
Standards suddenly are lax
When the children turn their backs

TV channels change and zap
Soap stars whinge and whine and yap
Volume turned up to the max
When the children turn their backs

The volume on the hi-fi rack's
Exploding like a thunderclap
Vibrating all the speaker stacks
When the children turn their backs

Dad thinks he's a trendy chap
Combat pants and baseball cap
Sings along to gangsta raps
When the children turn their backs

Mum has daughter's make-up pack
Bloodshot red and gothic black
Setting gel and styling wax
When the children turn their backs.

Fizzy pop and fast food snacks
Pizza slices, burger baps
Veg is in the rubbish sacks
When the children turn their backs

Mum and Dad know where it's at
More of this then more of that
They know how to relax . . .
When the children turn
    their backs!

Paul Cookson

Uncle Tobias

My uncle, Tobias Sebastian Prune
Was the first man from Wigan
To walk upon the moon!

Yanking his lunar barge-boots on,
Adjusting his life-support:
'One giant step for Wigan!'
is what he said and thought.

Up there he gathered data
From a great big dusty crater,
Collected funny globules
And lots of tiny nodules
Which he fed into a shredder
To test the moon for cheddar.

He hopped, he bounced, he floated
Like a great gas-filled balloon
About the unatmospheric mountains
Of his Wiganized moon,

In his tightly pumped-up space suit
With its set of bright and cute
Coloured lights that bleeped and blipped
As weightlessly he bounced
   and skipped
Back to his loony spacecraft
With all his loony lunar loot.

When he landed back in Lancashire,
'What was it like?' they said.
'It's made of black pudding,' he
   told them,
then trundled off to bed.

Matt Simpson

Uncle Frank

When we're asleep in bed,
My Uncle Frank unscrews his head.
He fixes on another one
And sets off for a night of fun.

It really gave me quite a jolt,
The first time that I saw the bolt,
Which Uncle proudly showed to me
In the cellar after tea.

He says the reasons for his fame
    Is that we share a famous name:
    Oh, I forgot to tell you mine,
      Our family's name
        is Frankenstein.

John Foster

Last Friday Near the Shed

I was digging and I found a box.
I opened it and found
an old red cape
a torn red mask
some mouldy red underpants
and a gun that shot red sauce.
So it was true.
My Grandad really was
THE TOMATO.

All those years when he told us stories
about holding up the bus
and making all the passengers get off
just so that he could spray them with red sauce
he was telling the truth.

Imagine that.
My Grandad: THE TOMATO.

So I wonder if my Grandma
really was
SQUID GIRL?

I'll get my spade.

Ian McMillan

My Theory About
My Dad

Where does Dad go to Friday nights?
And why does he come home so late?
Mam says he trots down to his 'local'
For a couple of drinks with his mates.

I only know that next morning
He has a lie-in until noon
Then he growls like an angry old lion
And grunts like a grumpy baboon;

He's a lumbering old hippopotamus
At least until teatime comes round,
Shambles about like an orang-utan
With arms hanging down to the ground.

Mam says he goes to 'The Elephant'
And I think that this is a clue:
My theory is: every Friday night
Dad goes studying down at the Zoo.

It's Animal Impersonation
The name of the course he is taking:
He wants to grunt on the telly!
My dad's a Big Star in the making!

Matt Simpson

The Neighbour
Without a Shadow

We never saw our neighbour in the daylight.
No one did. Who or what he was no one knew.
Some kids even doubted his existence.
'*No one lives in that house*', they'd whisper,
Staring at number forty with its unpainted door
Endlessly closed, and its grubby windows,
And velvet curtains thick with dust.
And you might have believed them
But for the sound of footsteps in the parlour,
And the nightly scraping of something
That sounded a bit like a coffin
Being pulled across the floor.

He was there alright, despite the fact
That even on the frostiest nights
No smoke rose from his chimney,
Despite the fact that no one ever called –
No postman, no milkman, no friends.
No one delivered even the barest necessities to his house,
But he was there, we were sure of it.
Shadowless. Sitting upright in the darkness,
Smiling his skeletal smile
As the months and the years passed,
And people passed by outside the house,
Whispering and doubting his existence,
Just as he wanted.

Brian Patten

My Dad's Shed

At the bottom
of the garden,
through the mist
and the dewy grass
is my dad's shed.

It's crooked and brown
and smells of
old, damp trees.

It doesn't look much.

But there is a crack,
a small sliver
in the door
and at night,
I can see in there.
Just.

It glows and sparkles inside,
like orange flames
and lightning
and shooting stars.

Things happen in there.

At night,
I watch from
my bedroom window
and I can see the splits
in the wood light up
like a Christmas tree.

I tell my dad,
excitedly, breathless,
but he just laughs
and winks
and ruffles my hair.

He knows that I know
about the shed,
he has seen the glitter
left on my hands
after I have picked
the amazing flowers
that grow by its door.

He looks at me
and his eyes twinkle
like the moon on the water.

And then he raises
his finger to his lips
and says, 'Sshh!'

John Prior

Next Door

My mum says
the woman next door
isn't a fly,

a huge bluebottle
rubbing six thin legs together
crawling upside down on the ceiling
sticking her long nose into the jam.

My mum says
that buzzing and whirring and humming
we hear each day through the wall
is only a Hoover.

If that's true, why
does her husband scuttle
over the floor on eight hairy legs
and build thick webs
in the dark cupboard under the stairs,

and why does Stan
her eldest son,
buy huge cans of Deadly Flykill?

When I next see her
zooming over the compost and dustbins
I'll have to ask her
just what's SWAT.

David Harmer

Secret Agent Mum

The other day I overheard
Mum talking on the phone
In a very serious voice,
Not her usual chatty tone.

I'm sure she said, 'Top Secret',
'Double agents' and 'spies',
'Undercover investigations'
And 'silencing bad guys'.

With my ear against the keyhole
Whilst crouching on the floor
Is how my mother found me
When she unlocked the kitchen door.

She barked down the receiver,
'It's not safe for me to speak.'
She said to me, 'Go to your room
Or you're grounded for a week.'

I thought it rather strange
For Mum to be that rude.
The weeks went by and she was back
To her usual cheerful mood.
But yesterday I took a call:
'Give me Double O Twenty-Three.'
Mum snatched the phone out of my hand
And said, 'That call's for me.'

John Coldwell

Gourmet Gran?

On Friday nights of every week
At Gran and Grandy's we go to sleep.
Last week as the clock struck one
A full moon through the window shone.

Downstairs we crept with silent tread
To find what lured us from our bed.
A light from out the kitchen glared
And through a door crack we both stared.

TV camera, gear and lights
And then the most bizarre of sights.
A tentacled alien with a greenish look
Said, 'Now some more from our Earthling cook.'

There was Gran at the kitchen table –
'Now my friends from Planet Mabel,
This week I've prepared for you
A special dish of human stew.

'Take two toes, half an ear, one eye,
Mince them together in a pie.
Bake with a juice that's red and wet,
Garnish with a smear of sweat.'

There was more of this until we fled
Quite revolted to our bed.
Next morning as soon as we could see
Gran and Grandy brought us tea.

'Morning, kids,' said Gran with a beam,
'I hope that cheese didn't make you dream.'
'Oh no it didn't,' was what we said,
But had we really been misled?

What about that mark on Grandy's
shirt?
Was it made by a piece of dirt,
Or perhaps a splash of mud?
Or was it ... actually ... ???

Redvers Brandling

Where Do All the Teachers Go?

Where do all the teachers go
When it's four o'clock?
Do they live in houses
And do they wash their socks?

Do they wear pyjamas
And do they watch TV?
And do they pick their noses
The same as you and me?

Do they live with other people?
Have they mums and dads?
And were they ever children?
And were they ever bad?

Did they ever, never spell right?
Did they ever make mistakes?
Were they punished in the corner
If they pinched the chocolate flakes?

Do they ever lose their hymn books?
Did they ever leave their greens?
Did they scribble on the desk tops?
Did they wear old dirty jeans?

I'll follow one back home today
I'll find out what they do
Then I'll put it in a poem
That they can read to you.

Peter Dixon

Wonderworks

Every morning after breakfast
Grandad's off like an arrow
To his shed where he's building
A flying wheelbarrow.
'It'll be brilliant,' he says
'A really good goer.
The perfect follow-up to my
Underwater lawnmower.'
He's got plans for jet-propelled skates
And then, a little later,
A supermarket hover-trolley
And a pocket refrigerator.
The sign that hangs on Grandad's shed
Says WONDERWORKS.
'Good name,' says Gran,
'It's a wonder if it works.'

Eric Finney

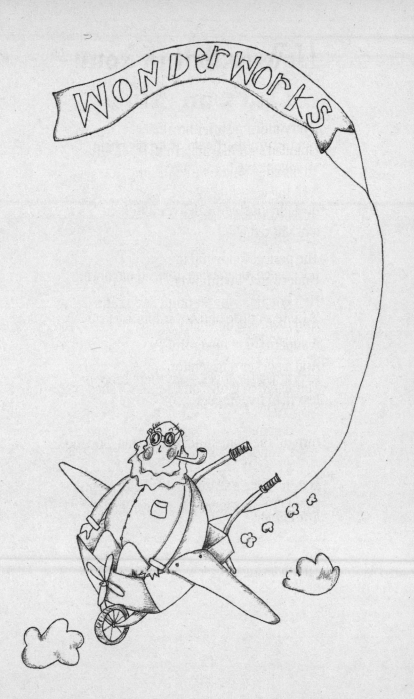

How to Tell if Your Dad's an Alien

can he turn the TV on, from his chair,
without using the remote

does the postbeing deliver letters in
a bright red UFO

does he go 'beep beep' instead of snoring

is there a bottle of fizzy sulphuric acid
in the fridge

look at Dad's gloves – are there more or
less than five fingers

turn off the light suddenly, is Dad glowing

does he have a season ticket to all Neptune
United's home games in his wallet?

Mike Johnson

The Tent by the Sea

I know an old woman called Mary McHutch
Who lives in a tent by the sea
Where she keeps a black box
Which she never unlocks,
And she's buried the old iron key.
She's buried the old iron key in the sand.

And deep in the damp dark it lies,
Whilst she taps and she knocks
On the old iron box
As she murmurs and mutters and sighs.

Oh, what have you got in your old iron box
In your tent by the sea, Miss McHutch?
Is it rubies and pearls, silk gowns for young girls,
Lockets and earrings and such?
Lockets and earrings and rubies and pearls
And birds made of gold in a tree?
Is it these that you keep
In the dark while you sleep,
Near the box in the tent by the sea?

In the box, in the tent, said Mary McHutch,
There are things that are not meant for show.
They stay unrevealed
When lips have been sealed –
There are secrets which no one must know.
There are secrets which no one must know, little friend,
And I've buried the old iron key,
The key that unlocks
My black, iron box
In the dark, in the tent, by the sea.

Jack Ousbey

Grandad's a Deep-Sea Diver

My grandad's got a secret life
Some say he's just a skiver.
But I know what he really does,
He's a daring deep-sea diver.

He keeps his wetsuit in the shed
And pretends he's down the pub,
Instead he's forty fathoms deep
Exploring the pond in a sub . . .

He's had some exciting moments,
Using his bi-focal specs
Finding unusual species,
Discovering old sunken wrecks.

Once Grandad swam into a shark.
It started a commotion.
It was at our local swimming pool
Not the middle of the ocean.

He'd fished for crabs and conger eels
But you wouldn't be impressed.
The only thing he caught was cold,
He'd been using his old string vest!

My grandma thinks she knows the man
Relaxing in his slippers,
And I would never tell her that
He prefers to wear his flippers!

Diane Humphrey

Weirdo

The secret's out, the secret's out,
My mother's weird without a doubt.

She races snails on Hampstead Heath
And tears up concrete with her teeth.

She smashes saucers in her room
And travels on a witches' broom.

She breeds cockroaches in her shed
And smashes housebricks with her head.

She wrestles with rhinos and grapples with gorillas
She mixes with muggers and madmen and killers.

She chews on rocks then spits 'em out,
She's Britain's most wanted lager lout.

She teaches tadpoles how to talk,
And eats her soup with a knife and fork.

She likes roast beef that's
covered in custard,
And pink bananas
smothered in mustard.

And yet at home with Dad and me
She looks as normal as can be.

You'd not expect that she was weird –
Apart, perhaps, from her purple beard . . .

Clive Webster

Gran at Night

At night
my gran
is a mole.
She burrows
beneath the lawn
beneath the flowerbed
under the fence
below the golf course
popping up
now and then
to leave
a heap of soil.
She catches
worms
grubs
woodlice;

she collects
leaves
dead petals
blades of grass.
My gran
is a mole
at night.

I know this:
she has soil
on her whiskers
in the morning.

Should I tell her?

Trevor Millum

Weatherman

Being a part-time weather maker
isn't easy for my Uncle Ron
    for a start
he's got seventeen and a half other jobs
most of which involve
sneezing, snoozing, snoring, burping
grumping, growling, scratching, laughing
      and leaping lightly across the stars.

      But every Friday
      he has a cup of tea with Auntie Lynda
      then potters down to his secret laboratory
      to make the weather for the weekend.

He boils sunshine in big glass bottles
molten reds and blazing scarlets
bright yellow bubbles bursting with gold
other times
  he brews up rain
in a steamy saucepan covered in clouds
that drip and drizzle down his windows.

Snow is hard, so is sleet
mixing up rain and ice in a bucket
hurts his hands
later he scatters scrunchy hailstones
like handfuls of gravel
        whips up a wind
that howls like wolves.

Like I said, he only works weekends
but he'll do special orders
        for friends of mine
so if there are any days you would like to arrange
for blazing sunshine or foggy damp
see me after reading this poem
I'll give you my uncle's secret phone number
as long as you don't
        tell anyone else.

David Harmer

Secret Service

My father has a secret job,
A job the whole world fears.
And when my father's hard at work,
He drives brave men to tears.

He sits in rooms so silent,
And makes sour, secret notes.
When he sees victims make some slip,
He grins and glowers and gloats.

He's done this job in secret
For over twenty years.
I daren't tell friends he does it,
For fear of spiteful sneers.

His well-paid work is hated.
It means he has no friends.
It means he sits there all alone
As each long workday ends.

'What does he do?' you ask me.
I beg you, please don't tell.
My dad's a Schools' Inspector.
Worse!
My mum is one as well!

John Kitching

Bob Bradley's Been Around

He lives in a bed of cabbages,
he sleeps with an old guitar.
He trusts his luck for his dinner,
his nightlight is a star.

He slips into town on Saturdays
to mingle with the masses.
There's poetry in each face he sees
and he always wears his glasses.

He rides the range on a tumbleweed
and sings out loud to the moon.
He's an old coyote with a history
he keeps in a silver spoon.

Linda Lee Welch

I Spy with My Little Eye

I'm not spying, just looking
with my super-magnifying telescope
out of my bedroom window
to the over-the-road-neighbour's house.

I'm not spying, just looking
when I should have been sleeping
I wish I'd not done it now,
wish I hadn't been peeping.

I'm not spying, just looking
with my super-magnifying telescope
my uncle gave it me at Christmas
he said don't look at the neighbour's house.

I'm not spying, just looking
but what I'm seeing is disgusting
do all grown-ups do this
all this guzzling and slurping?

I'm not spying, just looking
at the neighbours enjoying eating
scorpions and spiders, lizards and earwigs.
Are my neighbours aliens?

I've swapped my telescope
for a real live gerbil
    and cage
I'm watching my
    neighbours
don't have him
    for lunch.

Lesley Marshall

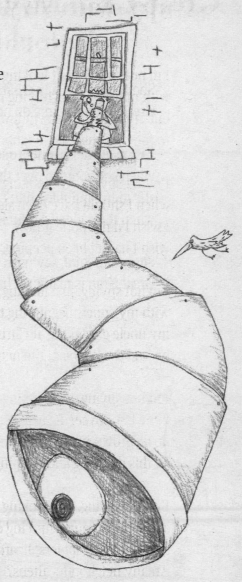

Great-Gran is Manic on Her Motorbike

Shout out loud, say what you like
Great-Gran is manic on her motorbike.

Last week her helmet touched the stars
when she zoomed over thirty cars
she didn't quibble, didn't fuss
when they added a double-decker bus.

Shout out loud, say what you like
Great-Gran is manic on her motorbike.

She's a headline-hunting,
    bike-stunting
wacky-wild-one-woman-
    show
she revs and roars to wild
    applause
there is no place her bike won't go
she gives them shivers jumping
    rivers
and balancing across high wires
with a cheer she changes gear
flies her bike through blazing tyres.

Shout out loud, say what you like
Great-Gran is manic on her motorbike.

She told me when she quits bike-riding
she's going to take up paragliding
I'll always be her greatest fan
my dazzling, daredevil, manic great-gran!

David Harmer

My Dad Was in His Room

all of a suddlington
he jumped off his bed
almost knocking over
the lamp that stood on the small table.

He heaved off his boots and socks,
throwing them wildly behind him.
Then he rolled up the legs of his jeans,
went outside and journeyed upwards
into the sky.

Everyone watched in amazement
as he paddled in the pink sunset.

Photographers click-clicked
as he dashed about from purple cloud
to orange cloud.

A vicar clasped his hands in prayer.

When he got back
he walked through the crowds of people
who had been watching him.

Television reporters tried to get him
to say a few words into their
microphones.
But he only smiled, and pointed at his toes
which were singing and dancing
all by themselves.

John Rice

When We're Asleep

Late at night when we're asleep
Tucked up tight in bed
We never know what Mum and Dad
Are doing then instead . . .

Sometimes racing rockets
Sometimes sailing seas
As pirates with the *Jolly Roger*
Flying in the breeze

Sometimes climbing mountains
Or scoring winning goals
Exploring unknown jungles
Or playing rock and roll

Then they're fighting monsters
Or beaming down on Mars
Casting magic spells
Or driving flying cars

Models on the catwalk
Parading latest trends
Relaxing in jacuzzis
Meeting famous friends

Taming lions, kissing sharks,
Riding dinosaurs,
Juggling prickly porcupines
To loud and wild applause

It's true they'd like to do these things
When we're tucked up in bed
But they're too tired because of us
When we're asleep then they're asleep . . .
So they dream them all instead.

Paul Cookson

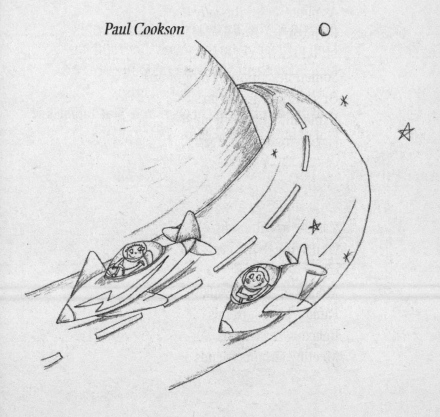

A Mother's Confession

(Or: What you have always suspected . . .)

As soon as you are asleep in bed
I unlock the secret cupboard
Where I keep all the chocolate
And I eat it and eat it and eat it.
I don't share it with anybody
And I don't give half a hoot about my teeth.

As soon as you are tucked all tidy in your bed
I put my feet up on the sofa – shoes still on,
Or if I take them off I don't undo the laces first,
Then I drink fizzy cans and eat crisps,
And practise blowing huge, round, pink bubbles
Out of hubba-bubba gum.

Once you're asleep
I watch *those* programmes on the telly
(The ones I always say are trash)
And I don't go to bed at a sensible time –
Even though I'm really, really tired.
I don't go because I'm a grown-up
And I can do what I like
And you can't stop me.
Ha. Ha. Ha.

Jan Dean

To Be Honest

To be honest
I don't really want to know.

It'll be disgusting, boring
Or probably both.

I'm not that bothered really
And I certainly don't want to waste my time thinking about it.

What grown-ups do
When I'm not looking has nothing to do with me.

And anyway, if they're so busy
They won't be bothering about what I'm doing, will they?

Ha.

Paul Cookson

taking my human for a walk

Poems chosen by Roger Stevens

Ever wondered what your pets think of you?
Taking my human for a walk reveals the truth at last!

A Sticky Riddle

It might seem obvious to you humans
But it puzzles me every day
If he wants the stick so badly
Why does he throw it away?

Roger Stevens

A selected list of poetry books
available from Macmillan Children's Books

The prices shown below are correct at the time of going to press.
However, Macmillan Publishers reserve the right to show new retail
prices on covers which may differ from those previously advertised.

Title	ISBN	Price
Taking My Human for a Walk Poems chosen by Roger Stevens	0 330 39871 7	£3.99
A Nest Full of Stars Poems by James Berry	0 330 39752 4	£4.99
Wallpapering the Cat Poems by Jan Dean	0 330 39903 9	£4.99
You're Not Going Out Like That! Poems chosen by Paul Cookson	0 330 39846 6	£3.99
The Teacher's Revenge Poems chosen by Brian Moses	0 330 39901 2	£3.99
One River Many Creeks Poems chosen by Valerie Bloom	0 333 96114 5	£9.99

All Macmillan titles can be ordered from our website,
www.panmacmillan.com, or from your local bookshop
and are also available by post from:

Bookpost
PO Box 29, Douglas, Isle of Man IM99 1BQ

Credit cards accepted. For details:
Telephone: 01624 836000
Fax: 01624 670923
E-mail: bookshop@enterprise.net
www.bookpost.co.uk

Free postage and packing in the UK.
Overseas customers: add £1 per book (paperback)
and £3 per book (hardback).